This **Child,**
EVERY **Child**

This Child, EVERY Child

A Book about the World's Children

Written by David J. Smith

Illustrated by Shelagh Armstrong

CitizenKid™

A collection of books that inform children about the
world and inspire them to be better global citizens

Kids Can Press

For all the children I've taught — hundreds in my own classrooms and countless thousands in other classrooms; for all the young children in my extended family, including Amelia Fay Stewart, Sophie and Caroline Lauriat, Lillie Anita Saunders, Greg and Jenna Mercer, David Merz, Prescott and Rozzie Nicoll, Eve Rose Gonson and others older and younger; for Dr. Frank Wang and his children; for Tam and Jin Ah; and, again and always, for Suzanne — DS

For my mother, Phyllis, who believed in me through the good times and the tough times, and for my wonderful family, Paul and Caden, for being so loving and understanding — SA

A NOTE FROM THE AUTHOR

Children do not choose to be exploited, to be forced to work or to fight in wars, to be separated from family and friends or to lose their homes, their health, property, security and safety, and yet millions of children around the world are routinely denied their basic rights. Children have rights — the same rights that all human beings have. These rights are set out in the United Nations Convention on the Rights of the Child, a global agreement created to safeguard the rights of children. This book may not be comfortable to read, but the topic — the presence or absence of basic human rights in the lives of children — is an important one.

Text © 2011 David J. Smith
Illustrations © 2011 Shelagh Armstrong

Kids Can Press acknowledges the financial support of the Government of Ontario, through the Ontario Media Development Corporation's Ontario Book Initiative; the Ontario Arts Council; the Canada Council for the Arts; and the Government of Canada, through the BPIDP, for our publishing activity.

Published in Canada by
Kids Can Press Ltd.
25 Dockside Drive
Toronto, ON M5A 0B5

Published in the U.S. by
Kids Can Press Ltd.
2250 Military Road
Tonawanda, NY 14150

www.kidscanpress.com

The artwork in this book was rendered in acrylic with digital textures.
The text is set in Bodoni.

Edited by Valerie Wyatt
Designed by Marie Bartholomew

This book is smyth sewn casebound.
Manufactured in Tseung Kwan O, NT Hong Kong, China, in 10/2010 by Paramount Printing Co. Ltd.

FSC
www.fsc.org
MIX
Paper from
responsible sources
FSC® C018769

CM 11 0 9 8 7 6 5 4 3 2 1

Library and Archives Canada Cataloguing in Publication

Smith, David J.
   This child, every child / written by David J. Smith ; illustrated by Shelagh Armstrong.

Includes bibliographical references.
ISBN 978-1-55453-466-1

1. Children—Juvenile literature. I. Armstrong, Shelagh, 1961– II. Title.

HQ767.9.S633 2011   j305.23   C2010-904767-2

Kids Can Press is a l'O̶r̶u̶s̶™ Entertainment company

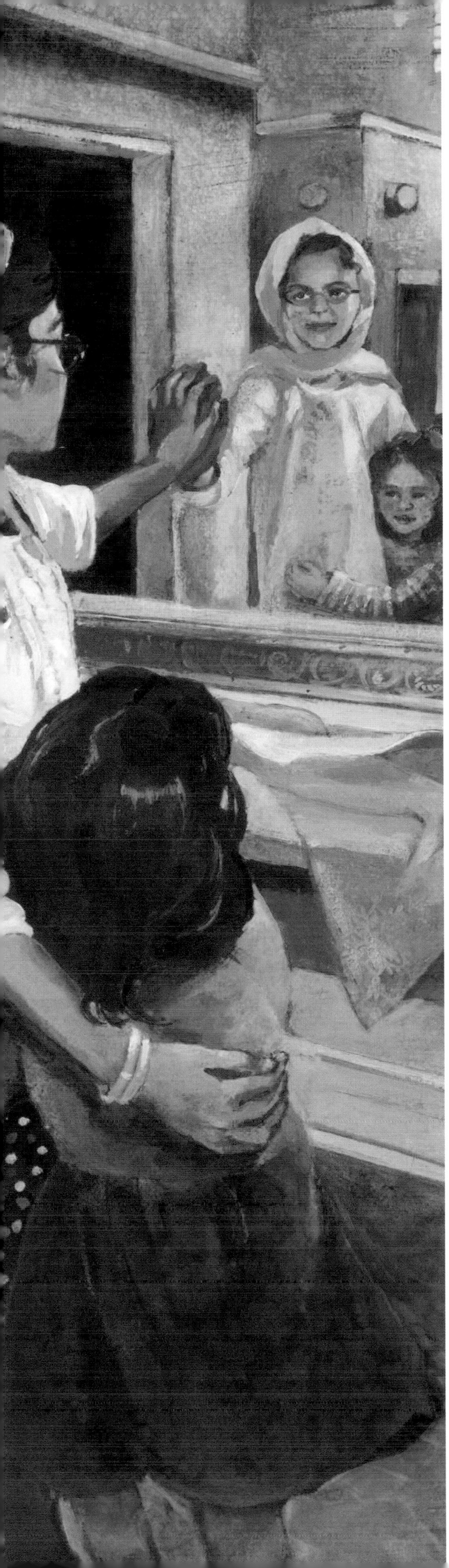

Contents

Foreword

Dear reader,

ONEXONE was founded with the philosophy that every single life is infinitely precious and that one by one, each person can make a difference. Our mission is to improve the lives of children in Canada, the USA and around the world with programs dedicated to five fundamental pillars: water, health, education, play and food.

We are excited to be associated with this latest title in the CitizenKid collection. I applaud David J. Smith's efforts to broaden children's understanding of how other kids live. Many of the readers of this book will be surprised and possibly even shocked by the conditions some children must endure — their lack of health care, basic education, adequate food. Readers will be moved by the stories of individual children, such as Sara from India, who is not allowed to go to school, unlike her brother, or Hakim, who lives in a village in Ethiopia where the drinking water comes from a single tap and villagers must share one flush toilet. But David Smith does not stop there. He provides readers with inspiring ideas on how they can learn more about the world's children and help change things for the better. Because, one by one, each child can make a difference.

Our journey at ONEXONE has reinforced my belief that helping another person is not a responsibility or an obligation but a privilege with great rewards. This is a message we must pass along to children, and it is a message that comes through loud and clear in This Child, Every Child.

When you have finished reading This Child, Every Child, *we invite you to discover the world of ONEXONE — the work we do and the humanity that drives us to achieve our goals. For more information about ONEXONE, please visit our website: www.onexone.org.*

Sincerely,

Joelle Berdugo-Adler
Founder, ONEXONE

Meet the children

You are one of more than 2.2 billion (2 200 000 000) children in the world. In fact, children make up about one-third of the world's population. That's a lot of children!

You may know about the children near you, in the same neighborhood, the same school, the same clubs and teams. But what about children in other countries? Are they like you? What are their lives like?

In this book, we will look at children around the world. We will also see how their lives measure up to the United Nations Convention on the Rights of the Child, an international agreement that was drawn up to protect children (see the box at the bottom of this page). And we will look at some individual children and how they live. Although their stories are imaginary, they do reflect the experiences of many children in their countries.

As you read, look for connections. For example, children who live in poverty, generally speaking, have shorter life spans than children elsewhere because they do not have adequate food supplies, medical care or access to schools and clean water. Other more fortunate children don't have to worry about these things — they have enough food, health services, schools and clean water. Not every child in a developing country is poor or sick; not every child in a wealthy country is rich or healthy. But there can be a relationship between where children live and what their lives are like, and knowing this can help us understand more about the children of the world.

Turn the page and let's begin to explore the world's children — where they live, how they live, and what their families and lives are like.

In 1989, the United Nations Convention on the Rights of the Child was agreed upon by all but two countries in the world — Somalia and the United States. (The United States is expected to formally agree to the Convention soon. Somalia does not currently have a government able to approve the Convention.)

The Convention sets out the rights that children have — such as protection from harm and discrimination, the right to life, health, education and survival and the right to be respected. Articles from the Convention appear in a box like this on each page. To see the entire Convention on the Rights of the Child, turn to page 32.

10

Children around the world

Children are not equally spread out around the world. Some countries have a low percentage of children, while others have a high percentage. Of the 30 countries with the lowest percentage of children, 27 are in Europe. Of the 30 countries with the highest percentage of children, 25 are in Africa.

Ada (a name that means "firstborn daughter") is one of those African children. She is 10 years old and lives with her family in a small, mud-walled house near Niamey, the capital of Niger (nee-ZHER). Here we see her as she sits in the afternoon shade of a tree outside her house, making a basket.

Ada is the oldest child in her family of four children. They all go to the village school, where they are given one good meal a day. Without this school meal, they might have just one bowl of millet porridge a day at home. In Niger, only one-third of the children go to school — and only a small proportion of those children are girls. So Ada is one of the lucky ones.

Niger has the highest percentage of children under 15 of any country in the world — about 50 percent. By comparison, 30 percent are that young in Indonesia; 25 percent in China; 22 percent in the United States; and 15 percent in Bulgaria. In Japan, which has the lowest percentage of young people anywhere, only 13 percent are children under 15.

Children in many African countries, including Niger, often face special challenges. This is because countries with a high percentage of children often have a hard time providing services for all of them. Education, medical care and other resources are expensive, and, therefore, not widely available. Children may not get what they need to thrive or even just survive.

> The government has a responsibility to make sure your rights are protected. They must help your family to protect your rights and create an environment where you can grow and reach your potential. (Article 4)

Children and their families

Families come in all sizes. Many are made up of one or two parents and one or more children. In other families, aunts, uncles, cousins and grandparents share the same home. Let's compare two very different families.

Eleven-year-old Lucas lives in Ystad [EW-stad], a city in southern Sweden. He shares his home with his parents and his older sister. Since both of his parents work, and his sister is often visiting her friends, Lucas regularly spends time alone at home.

Mamadou is also 11. He lives in a village near Bamako, the capital of Mali, in northern Africa. Mamadou's father has two wives, who together have four boys and two girls. The average family in Mali has 6.6 children. In the family home, there are also lots of other relatives — aunts, uncles and cousins — all of whom are considered part of the family and live with the family most of the year. It's not unusual for as many as 10 or 12 people to live in Mamadou's home, and he is rarely alone. In fact, he would consider it odd to be on his own — he is used to having family members around him all the time.

Lucas's family is just slightly smaller than the world average of 2.6 children, and Mamadou's family is much larger. Family size varies from country to country. Many countries in Africa and Asia have an average family size of between five and seven children, or even more. Parents in these countries often have more children because they know that not all of the children will survive. They may also want more children to help support the family and to look after them when they get old. And sometimes, aunts, uncles and grandparents share a home to keep the family together and to save money.

Many countries all over the world are encouraging smaller families because large populations can be hard to care for. As a result, family size has been shrinking steadily around the world over the last 20 years.

✿✿✿✿✿✿✿✿✿✿✿✿✿✿✿✿✿✿✿✿

> **You have the right to live with your parent(s) unless it is bad for you. You have the right to live with a family who cares for you. (Article 9)**

13

Children at home

Around the world, there are hundreds of different types of homes. Dwellings range from single-family homes, to multifamily apartments and houses, to movable dwellings such as tents, trailers and yurts (tentlike structures covered with felt). Even houseboats are home for some children.

Ling lives on a boat in Aberdeen Harbour, in Hong Kong. Her city is one of the most densely populated places on Earth, and people sometimes struggle to find homes. In Aberdeen Harbour, there are several thousand boats, and on each boat, one or more large families. Ling and her family are surrounded by a big, busy city with its roaring traffic, colorful boats, flags and banners, and by the smells of fish, cooking and seawater. There are people everywhere, all the time.

Many of the boat dwellers go to sea every day to fish, but others live on boats that do not leave their moorings. Some people may spend their entire lives without ever setting foot on land, while others shuttle by boat to the city for work. In many cases, several boats are tied together at a dock, and people walk across other people's boats on their way to dry land.

Ling and her brother walk across seven boats to get to a dock and then walk to school. Their boat home never leaves its mooring, and Ling's mother and grandparents rarely leave the boat. Instead, they depend on the children to bring home food for the family's meals.

Ling is lucky. Although her home is unusual, it is still a home, where she receives love and care from her family. There are more than 100 million children in the world who have no home. Nearly 40 percent of all homeless children live in Latin America and 20 percent live in India. They spend their lives on the streets, alone or as part of a street family, or in an institution, such as an orphanage.

You have the right to food, clothing, a safe place to live and to have your basic needs met. You should not be disadvantaged so that you can't do many of the things other kids do. (Article 27) You have the right to special care and help if you cannot live with your parents. (Article 20)

Children's health

If you have access to health care, clean water, adequate food and a healthy environment, you are better off than many children in the world. Children who lack even one of these things can be in danger.

Hakim is a 10-year-old boy who lives with his mother and sisters on the outskirts of Sendafa, a small town not far from Addis Ababa, the capital of Ethiopia. Hakim attends a school that provides a school lunch, so he has adequate nutrition. Half of the children in Ethiopia are undernourished because their families cannot afford enough food.

The school has a visiting doctor, who gives students vaccinations to prevent diseases such as polio, measles and meningitis. But one-third of Ethiopian children are not immunized against diseases. Hakim also has a sleeping net to prevent mosquitoes that carry malaria from infecting him. If he did become infected, the doctor would give him medicine to stop the malaria. In areas affected by malaria around the world, only about 15 percent of children sleep under nets, and fewer than 40 percent receive any treatment if they get the disease.

When it comes to a healthy environment, Hakim is less fortunate. Air quality in Sendafa is fairly good, but water quality is not, and sanitation in the village is primitive. There is a single outside water tap for Hakim and his neighbors, but in the dry season, the water may dry up, forcing people to travel long distances to find water. And there is only one flush toilet for his whole neighborhood, which is shared by many people. In Ethiopia, only about one-third of the people have access to safe drinking water, and about one-tenth have access to sanitation facilities.

But Hakim is still lucky compared to other children. He, at least, has access to some of the resources needed to be healthy. The lives and futures of many children now at risk can improve with health care, clean water, adequate food and a healthy environment.

You have the right to the best health care possible, safe water to drink, nutritious food, a clean and safe environment, and information to help you stay well. (Article 24)

Children on the move

You may have moved from one city to another or even to a new country. Children often move to new places, usually with their families. The move may be for safety, because of a parent's work, to be nearer to relatives or schools or even to follow migratory animals.

Some children move alone. They may be kidnapped or sold by their families for money or food — their families may believe better opportunities await the children in other places. These children may find themselves far from home, forced to be domestic servants, lightweight jockeys on camels or horses, workers in factories or beggars.

No one knows how many children move voluntarily or because they have to. But we do know some of their stories.

Chun Hei is a six-year-old girl who was born in Korea to a very young mother who could not take care of her. As a baby, Chun Hei was put up for adoption with an international organization. She was adopted by an American couple who flew to Korea to meet her and bring her home with them to San Francisco. Chun Hei is now in grade one.

Temani is a five-year-old boy from Yemen who moved with his family to a new village to avoid fighting between different tribes in his birth village. But the people in the new village harassed Temani's family because they were different.

After his father was injured and his brother badly beaten in a fight, the family applied for refugee status in the Netherlands, and they were accepted. (A refugee is a person who has been forced to leave his or her home and to live in another country.) Temani's family now lives in Groningen, in northern Holland.

Juan is seven years old. He was born in Santa Ana, in northwest Mexico. His parents were very unhappy with conditions in Mexico, so they applied and received permission to immigrate to the United States. Juan's father is now a farmworker in California, but the family is still struggling. They have to move often so that Juan's father can find work. As a result, Juan's schooling gets interrupted. They live in crowded conditions, eat inadequately and rarely get the health care they need. There are organizations that watch out for children like Juan. They do what they can to give Juan and others like him a better chance.

☆ ☆ ☆ ☆ ☆ ☆ ☆ ☆ ☆ ☆ ☆ ☆ ☆ ☆ ☆ ☆ ☆

If you live in a different country than your parents do, you have the right to be together in the same place. (Article 10) You have the right to be protected from kidnapping. (Article 11) You have the right to special protection and help if you are a refugee (if you have been forced to leave your home and live in another country), as well as all the rights in this Convention. (Article 22)

Children at school

Around the world, nearly 80 million children do not go to school — some because they have to work, some because of wars and conflicts where they live and some simply because there is no school nearby.

Even so, most of the world's children do learn to read and write at school or at home or from others. By age 25, about 90 percent of males and 85 percent of females are literate, which means they can read and write.

Many countries do better than this, but other countries do not. Most of the world's illiterate adults (those who cannot read and write) live in just a small number of countries. In China, for example, only 7 percent of the people are illiterate. But because China has so many people, that means there are 92 million Chinese people who are illiterate. Here are the percentages for a few other countries and the approximate number of illiterate people: Bangladesh 47.5 percent are illiterate (85 million people); Pakistan 46 percent (83 million); India 37 percent (421 million); Egypt 34 percent (28 million); Nigeria 28 percent (42 million); Brazil 10 percent (19 million); and Indonesia 8 percent (18 million).

Salmaa is a 10-year-old girl who lived for many years in a village near Shiraz, in southern Iran. While most Iranian girls are taught to read, many do not go beyond primary school, especially outside the big cities. Salmaa's family struggled to find work, and this meant that Salmaa had to leave school to do household chores and look after the younger children. But she dreamed of going back to school and becoming a nurse or doctor.

Because opportunities for work and education were scarce in Iran, Salmaa's family decided to move to Canada. While it is cooler and rainier in their new country, the family has settled in and Salmaa is making friends. Best of all, she is going to school. In Canada, almost 100 percent of school-aged children go to school. Salmaa still hopes to be a nurse or doctor, and now her chances are much better.

You have the right to a good quality education. You should be encouraged to go to school to the highest level you can. (Article 28) Your education should help you use and develop your talents and abilities. It should also help you learn to live peacefully, protect the environment and respect other people. (Article 29)

Are boys and girls treated equally?

The simple answer to this question is no. For the most part, in most of the world, boys and girls are not treated equally. Girls are denied opportunities — to go to school, to make choices about the kind of work they do, or to make their own decisions about their lives. Sometimes — although not often — it is boys who are discriminated against. Many countries and organizations are working to change things.

Let's look at two families.

Amir and Sara are brother and sister, eight and nine years old, who live in a village near Chennai, in southeast India. The custom in their community is that boys are treated differently from girls — for example, the women and girls eat last and least so that the men and boys will have more.

Amir attends the local school, while Sara stays home and helps with the household chores, walking long distances with her mother every day to fetch water and firewood. Although Sara is only nine years old, she is engaged to be married, an arrangement her parents made when she was an infant. The law says she must be 18 to marry, but in her village about half the girls between 10 and 14 are married. Her brother Amir will finish school and may continue his education or take a job. He will be able to select and marry a bride of his choice, with the approval of his mother and father.

Karun and Lalasa are also brother and sister and also eight and nine years old. Their family moved from India to a suburb of London, England, when the children were small. They both attend the local school. In England, the law requires boys and girls to have equal opportunities for schooling, food, jobs and medical care, and to freely make their own choices about their lives.

Of the four children, it is Sara who has the fewest choices, and this may put her at risk later on. For example, without an education, she may find it difficult to get work and support herself if she needs to. Worldwide, girls and women have fewer opportunities than boys and men throughout their lives. As a result, there are more women than men who live in poverty. About 70 percent of the world's poor are women.

✷✷✷✷✷✷✷✷✷✷✷✷✷✷✷✷✷✷✷

All children have these rights ... no matter whether they are a boy or a girl ... (Article 2) Your family has the responsibility to help you learn to exercise your rights, and to ensure that your rights are protected. (Article 5)

Children and work

Nearly 220 million children between the ages of 5 and 17 work at full-time jobs. Many work for families — their own families or other families. They do unpaid or poorly paid work, often farming or household labor, rather than going to school. But one-third of all working children are in hazardous jobs that put them at risk of accidents.

Gabriel is nine and lives with his family in Guatemala City, the capital of Guatemala. His older brother attends school, but there is no money to send Gabriel, and so he works at whatever jobs he can. Recently, he found work in a fireworks factory, a dangerous job because of all the chemicals and the possibility of explosions. About one-quarter of all children in Central and South America work, and 18 million of them are under the age of 14. Most work in factories or on farms for very low wages.

Nasir, age nine, and Omar, age ten, live in Pakistan and work in a rug factory. The factory boss likes having boys work for him — boys are cheaper to hire than men, and their small hands are well suited to the delicate work. However, the conditions are not good for children — they work six or seven days a week and must stay in one position for many hours at a time. In Pakistan, 8.6 million children under the age of 18 work rather than go to school, and 1.4 million of these children are under age 10.

Eight-year-old Kumba lives with her family in Liberia, outside the capital of Monrovia. The closest school is far away, and the family has no money to send Kumba or her sister there. Also, Kumba's parents have decided to keep the girls home to help fetch water and firewood, tend the garden, prepare meals, clean and help with the washing. In Liberia, about one-third of school-aged children do not attend school. Instead, they labor on family farms and rubber plantations, in mines, on fishing boats and in fish plants, and loading and unloading trucks. They also work as market or street vendors, as beggars or as household servants.

You have the right to protection from work that harms you, and is bad for your health and education. If you work, you have the right to be safe and paid fairly. (Article 32)

Children at play

Children around the world do a lot of the same things in their free time, but there are differences from country to country.

Jack is 10 years old and lives in Brisbane, Australia. Leisure and fun are highly valued in Australia. When he is not in school, Jack watches television or videos, reads and plays computer games. Three-fifths of children in Australia also participate in organized sports. Jack plays cricket and soccer on neighborhood teams. He enjoys television sports shows — he watches cricket, football and rugby.

Pramana is also 10 and lives in Denpasar, on the island of Bali in Indonesia. In his country, there is less leisure time. Children must study their religion and religious practices, and celebrations take up a large part of Pramana's life. After school, he usually has only a short time to relax or to play soccer with his friends or a game with his sister. The games often include kite flying and marbles. When Pramana watches television, like Jack, he usually watches sports.

No matter where they live in the world, children do many of the same kinds of things for fun. They take part in team and group activities, such as organized sports, clubs and Scouting. And they do informal things, such as watch television or play with friends.

When children around the world are asked what sport they most like to participate in, swimming is number one in every country except India. There, cricket is number one. After swimming come soccer, cycling, basketball and athletic events, such as running, jumping and throwing.

However, when children are asked what their favorite leisure activity is, playing with toys always comes out on top. Worldwide, the most popular toys are model cars and trucks, dolls, building blocks and toy animals.

All children play games with friends. Among these games are variations on "Capture the Flag." In Congo, for example, the game is called *Bokwele*, and players steal rags from plastic hoops. Tag games are popular everywhere, too. In Brazil's *Gato Doente* and South Africa's *Kameshi Ne Mpuku*, a child, pretending to be a cat, is "it." The "cat" chases another child who pretends to be a rat.

At least 500 million children use the Internet regularly. When asked what they like to do on the Internet, children usually answer: playing and downloading music, e-mailing, surfing, playing games, messaging friends, visiting chat rooms and doing homework. The number one search term used by children is "games."

☆☆☆☆☆☆☆☆☆☆☆☆☆☆☆☆

You have the right to play and rest. (Article 31)

Children and war

Children all over the world are affected by war. In the last 10 years, more than 2 million children have been killed in wars, 1 million have been orphaned, and 12 million have been left homeless. Also, long after wars have ended, many children are killed or injured by land mines and other explosives that have been left behind. Three to four thousand children are maimed or die each year because of these explosives.

Some children are drawn into wars as soldiers. Sam, a young teenaged boy in Sierra Leone, was abducted from his family and forced to join the Small Boys Unit of a rebel army. He managed to escape after a few months and made his way home, but now he suffers from nightmares and is always fearful. With the help of UNICEF and other organizations, Sam is getting the care he needs to be a normal boy.

The armies of more than 50 nations have children under age 18. Most are age 16 or 17 and must have their parents' permission to enlist. But there are also about 300 000 young children who are part of rebel armies. They are trained to kill or to be servants — they gather firewood, do laundry, run errands or cook. The youngest child soldiers are thought to be about seven years old.

Many of these young soldiers have been kidnapped from their families, as Sam was. But sometimes children join armies willingly. They may join because they are hungry, hoping to get money or food to take back to their families. If their parents die and there is nobody to care for them, they may see the army as a new home. They may even join thinking it will be an exciting adventure. It never is. Children in war suffer abuse and are often forced to kill out of fear of punishment.

The United Nations is trying to stop the use of child soldiers around the world. Member countries have agreed to stop using child soldiers, although many national armies, such as those in the United States and Canada, still permit youth under 18 to join up, with their parents' consent. And there are still rebel armies around the world that continue to use even younger children.

You have the right to protection and freedom from war. Children under 15 cannot be forced to go into the army or take part in a war. (Article 38)

Children and the future

It takes about 10 seconds to read Article 42 in the box on the next page. In that time, 40 new babies will have been born somewhere in the world. Every second of every day, four more children are added to the world's population of over 2.2 billion children.

Some of these children will have good health care and schools. They will be cared for by their families and have enough food to eat and a place to call home. But many others will not be so fortunate. Despite the United Nations Convention on the Rights of the Child, which sets out the rights children have to a healthy, secure life, many children will fall behind. Every day, more than 30 000 children under the age of five die from diseases that could be prevented, and millions of children work in hazardous and harmful conditions. Unfortunately, most of those children are found in developing countries, mainly in Africa and South Asia.

Compared to 10 years ago, more children live in poverty today, and more children find themselves living in unstable or violent surroundings. But there is some good news. A large number of organizations, such as the United Nations and aid organizations like Save the Children and SOS Children's Villages, are working on these problems. Because they know — we all know — that children are the future.

The future of the world depends on today's children, and the world needs to make sure that all children — including you — get an education and develop safely, happily and successfully into adults. Then communities and countries will have citizens and leaders who can care for the next generation of children.

How well are governments and organizations doing? Let's look at one last child.

Cana, a 10-year-old girl who lives near Baku, Azerbaijan, close to the Caspian Sea, was recently living in poverty and despair as a beggar. She has a disability — her left leg never developed properly — and she has to use a wheelchair or crutches to get around. Cana was recruited into a UNICEF-supported program called the Youth Azeri Parcel Service, which is a delivery service run by disabled children. The deliveries are made by orphans and other children in need. The program provides a service to the businesses in Baku and provides income — and hope — for the children involved in it.

Cana now has skills and knowledge that will help her find work as an adult. She also has a small amount of money for clothes, food and other purchases. And she no longer spends her days begging and hungry.

With care, support and some good luck, Ada, Lucas, Mamadou, Ling, Hakim, Chun Hei, Temani, Juan, Salmaa, Amir, Sara, Karun, Lalasa, Gabriel, Nasir, Omar, Kumba, Jack, Pramana, Sam, Cana and all the other children of the world will become the wise adults and responsible leaders of the future.

All children have these rights, no matter who they are, where they live, what their parents do, what language they speak, what their religion is, whether they are a boy or a girl, what their culture is, whether they have a disability, whether they are rich or poor... (Article 2) You have the right to know your rights! Adults should know about these rights and help you learn about them, too. (Article 42)

Children's rights

The articles in boxes at the bottom of the pages in this book are from the United Nations Convention on the Rights of the Child. The Convention is a long list of rights that members of the United Nations agreed to accept. Most importantly, it is "non-negotiable." This means that all countries belonging to the United Nations agreed to follow every article in full.

Here is the whole document in a special child friendly version prepared by UNICEF Canada. As you read through the articles, think about your own life. You have the same rights as all the children in this book, but you may find it eye-opening to compare your life with theirs. Are your rights mostly respected by the adults in your life? What might your life be like if that were not so?

✹ ✹ ✹

The United Nations Convention on the Rights of the Child in Child Friendly Language

Preface: "Rights" are things every child should have or be able to do. All children have the same rights. These rights are listed in the United Nations Convention on the Rights of the Child. Almost every country has agreed to these rights. All the rights are connected to each other, and all are equally important. Sometimes we have to think about rights in terms of what is the best for children in a situation and what is critical to life and protection from harm. As you grow, you have more responsibility to make choices and exercise your rights.

Article 1: Everyone under 18 has these rights.

Article 2: All children have these rights, no matter who they are, where they live, what their parents do, what language they speak, what their religion is, whether they are a boy or a girl, what their culture is, whether they have a disability, whether they are rich or poor. No child should be treated unfairly on any basis.

Article 3: All adults should do what is best for you. When adults make decisions, they should think about how their decisions will affect children.

Article 4: The government has a responsibility to make sure your rights are protected. They must help your family to protect your rights and create an environment where you can grow and reach your potential.

Article 5: Your family has the responsibility to help you learn to exercise your rights, and to ensure that your rights are protected.

Article 6: You have the right to be alive.

Article 7: You have the right to a name, and this should be officially recognized by the government. You have the right to a nationality (to belong to a country).

Article 8: You have the right to an identity — an official record of who you are. No one should take this away from you.

Article 9: You have the right to live with your parent(s), unless it is bad for you. You have the right to live with a family who cares for you.

Article 10: If you live in a different country than your parents do, you have the right to be together in the same place.

Article 11: You have the right to be protected from kidnapping.

Article 12: You have the right to give your opinion, and for adults to listen and take it seriously.

Article 13: You have the right to find out things and share what you think with others, by talking, drawing, writing or in any other way unless it harms or offends other people.

Article 14: You have the right to choose your own religion and beliefs. Your parents should help you decide what is right and wrong, and what is best for you.

Article 15: You have the right to choose your own friends and join or set up groups, as long as it isn't harmful to others.

Article 16: You have the right to privacy.

Article 17: You have the right to get information that is important to your well-being, from radio, newspapers, books, computers and other sources. Adults should make sure that the information you are getting is not harmful, and help you find and understand the information you need.

Article 18: You have the right to be raised by your parent(s), if possible.

Article 19: You have the right to be protected from being hurt and mistreated, in body or mind.

Article 20: You have the right to special care and help if you cannot live with your parents.

Article 21: You have the right to care and protection if you are adopted or in foster care.

Article 22: You have the right to special protection and help if you are a refugee (if you have been forced to leave your home and live in another country), as well as all the rights in this Convention.

Article 23: You have the right to special education and care if you have a disability, as well as all the rights in this Convention, so that you can live a full life.

Article 24: You have the right to the best health care possible, safe water to drink, nutritious food, a clean and safe environment, and information to help you stay well.

Article 25: If you live in care or in other situations away from home, you have the right to have these living arrangements looked at regularly to see if they are the most appropriate.

Article 26: You have the right to help from the government if you are poor or in need.

Article 27: You have the right to food, clothing, a safe place to live and to have your basic needs met. You should not be disadvantaged so that you can't do many of the things other kids can do.

Article 28: You have the right to a good quality education. You should be encouraged to go to school to the highest level you can.

Article 29: Your education should help you use and develop your talents and abilities. It should also help you learn to live peacefully, protect the environment and respect other people.

Article 30: You have the right to practice your own culture, language and religion — or any you choose. Minority and indigenous groups need special protection of this right.

Article 31: You have the right to play and rest.

Article 32: You have the right to protection from work that harms you, and is bad for your health and education. If you work, you have the right to be safe and paid fairly.

Article 33: You have the right to protection from harmful drugs and from the drug trade.

Article 34: You have the right to be free from sexual abuse.

Article 35: No one is allowed to kidnap or sell you.

Article 36: You have the right to protection from any kind of exploitation (being taken advantage of).

Article 37: No one is allowed to punish you in a cruel or harmful way.

Article 38: You have the right to protection and freedom from war. Children under 15 cannot be forced to go into the army or take part in war.

Article 39: You have the right to help if you've been hurt, neglected or badly treated.

Article 40: You have the right to legal help and fair treatment in the justice system that respects your rights.

Article 41: If the laws of your country provide better protection of your rights than the Articles in this Convention, those laws should apply.

Article 42: You have the right to know your rights! Adults should know about these rights and help you learn about them, too.

Articles 43 to 54: These articles explain how governments and international organizations like UNICEF will work to ensure children are protected with their rights.

Learning more about the world's children

✴ ✴ ✴

This Child, Every Child uses statistics and stories to look at the lives of children around the world. As young readers will discover, there are striking disparities in the way children live. Some children lack opportunities that many readers of this book take for granted. Less fortunate children may have intermittent or nonexistent health care and poor access to education or to such basics as adequate food and clean drinking water. Their lives may be disrupted by war or their families torn apart by economic hardship.

One way governments have tried to safeguard children is to establish a set of universal rights, the United Nations Convention on the Rights of the Child. The rights of children are especially important because children are more vulnerable, more easily exploited and less able to control their own destinies. The Convention is an effort to help people understand and respect children's rights and to ensure that children worldwide have equal opportunities.

Learn more and keep on learning

There is so much for children to learn about other children in the world and the ways they can help. Here are some topics to prompt discussion.

• Invite people from other countries and cultures to visit. Encourage children to ask questions. Here are some questions to get them going. Do they have other questions?

How do people greet each other in the visitor's country? (Shake hands? Bow? Embrace?) How do they part? Are there any taboos? For example, in some cultures it is wrong to touch a person on the head or to show the soles of your feet when sitting.

When do children give or accept gifts? What gifts are considered appropriate or inappropriate?

Are children usually present at social gatherings? Are women? Are the elderly?

How are public sanitation, hygiene and garbage dealt with?

How do children spend their leisure time? How do adults spend theirs?

What are the important holidays and how are they observed?

• Older children can discuss issues that have no simple answers. Here are some examples:

If child labor puts some children at risk, should we boycott products made by children — or will this just make things worse for those children?

What vaccinations have children had? Perform a school or family census. About 20 percent of the world's people have no immunization against any disease and no access to health care of any kind. Why do children think this might be? Ask them to propose solutions.

Many refugees escaping from war or drought or other calamities around the world are children, and they may be cut off from home, an education and often from their own families. How can those of us who are more fortunate help? What organizations can we work or raise money for?

• Ask children to imagine that they are one of the children described in this book. What would life be like if they were Ada or Mamadou or any of the others? Ask children to write a diary for one day in the life of their child, describing getting up, what happens to them during the day, how they get their meals and so on. An extra challenge would be to pick a "special" day — maybe a birthday, the first day of school or a visit to a doctor. Older children might want to write a play. At http://www.mapping.com, there is a bibliography of books about the children of the world, including books of games, songs and activities. Children can include some of these in their play.

• Have children assemble a global village of housing styles. "Home" can mean different things to different people. And what about the homeless? Ask children to imagine what it would be like to live on the streets for just one week. What would they eat? Where would they go to the bathroom and wash? Where would they sleep?

• Think about water. Chart water use in your country and make comparisons to other countries. Brainstorm ways to reduce your own water use. After all, there is only "one well" of shared water that must support all humanity. You can help this discussion of water along by "turning off" your home or school water supply for an hour or two, except for one washroom. (You don't actually have to turn anything off, just post "off limits" signs on taps and toilets.) Discuss children's experience of this "water shortage."

Think about water quality. Unsafe water is a big issue for the world's children. Contaminated water contributes to diarrhea and other illnesses. An estimated 3.5 million children die each year from these diseases.

Think about other water issues. For example, in some countries, girls and women are expected to fetch water a great distance from their homes. This task cuts into (and sometimes eliminates) time that could be spent in school or engaging in other productive activities.

Take action

There are lots of ways that children can get involved and help create lasting changes in the lives of less fortunate children. Here are just a few examples. You and your children can probably think of others.

• Find an organization that supports the rights, safety or health of children in your community or elsewhere in the world. Organize fund-raising activities or brainstorm ways to make people more aware of the issues.

• Ask children how they might help less privileged children who live in their own community. For example, food banks often need donations of canned food. Family shelters might appreciate receiving books and toys. Children can also donate their time. Look for volunteer opportunities at after-school or weekend programs.

• Help Habitat for Humanity build a house near you. Although children under 16 are not permitted on construction sites, they can participate in other ways. There are programs to raise money for homes, student-initiated advocacy weeks on housing issues and more. See http://www.habitat.org/youth programs/

• If your school has a video camera, write and produce some public-service announcements about the issues of homelessness and the rights and lives of children. Then take the videos to your local TV station. By law, stations that show advertising have to show a certain percentage of public service announcements. A TV station may decide to show one of your videos or possibly do a more polished production.

• Red Hand Day, February 12, is a worldwide effort led by young people to end the practice of forcing children to become child soldiers. There are many activities, including putting red ink on hands to make red palm prints. Children can make a poster of the prints or send their individual prints to an organization that collects red hands to send to the United Nations. Visit http://www.redhandday.org/ or enter "red hand day" into a search engine to find more information.

• Put on a "starvation meal," such as the Hunger Banquets that Oxfam sponsors, to help children understand global hunger. Participants draw tickets (or marbles or chips) from a bag. Those with a white ticket get plain rice; a red ticket (of which there are only a few) means plain rice with sauce; a blue ticket (a tiny percentage) means a three-course meal served by others at a table set with a tablecloth. The banquet itself is not the point, but rather the discussion afterward and the development of action plans. There are many online resources to help with putting on this kind of event.

It can be very challenging to help a child understand the complex, confusing and sometimes frightening issues surrounding the children highlighted in this book. Children need to know that change is possible. In the last 150 years, public health measures have eradicated many diseases, dramatically reduced infant mortality and significantly increased average life expectancy. Policies and agreements, such as the Convention on the Rights of the Child, have empowered governments and organizations to solve other problems, such as reducing the impact of poverty, increasing access to education and health care and curbing the exploitation of children at work and during war.

Children themselves have amazing power to change things. Children have helped raise money for wells where freshwater is scarce, for farmers to get their crops to market, for books or supplies for needy schools and children and for efforts to support the health and well-being of children all over the world.

As adults, we need to model the behavior we want to see. We need to encourage children to feel as passionate about the issues as we do and to help us do something that can make a difference in the world. How do we do that? We can volunteer with our children, and we can tell them about our own beliefs and about the people who have inspired us. And we can show our children that we are vitally interested in what is happening in the rest of the world. To make a difference, our mantra must always be this: Change is possible.

A note on sources

Many Web sites and print sources were used to compile the data for this book. I generally began my research using Web sites of child-related organizations, and then I verified the data with print sources. The organizations whose Web sites I used, and their top-level Web addresses, are listed below, followed by citations for my print sources. Not all sources agreed. If necessary, averages or extrapolations have been made from related information.

Web sites:
Population Reference Bureau:
http://www.prb.org
This site links to the *World Population Data Sheet* and other useful publications.

UNICEF Web sites:
http://www.unicef.org

The State of the World's Children reports:
http://www.unicef.org/sowc
   Maternal and Newborn Health (2009)
   Women and Children (2007)
   Excluded and Invisible (2006)
   Childhood Under Threat (2005)
   Girls, Education and Development (2004)

Progress for Children reports:
http://www.unicef.org/progressforchildren

A World Fit for Us (2007):
http://www.unicef.org/publications/index_42122.html

UNICEF also sponsors several other very useful Web sites. For example, their site http://www.childinfo.org is a good source for health and other issues pertaining to women and children.

The United Nations Office for the Coordination of Humanitarian Affairs (OCHA) Web sites:
http://ochaonline.un.org
This site links to the *Compilation of United Nations Resolutions on Humanitarian Assistance* (2009), annual reports and many other publications.

ReliefWeb:
http://www.reliefweb.int
OCHA administers this site, which contains information on worldwide emergencies and the humanitarian response to those events.

Map Centre:
http://www.reliefweb.int/rw/rwb.nsf/doc114?OpenForm
Within ReliefWeb, Map Centre is a useful and important source for country and regional maps. By showing the locations of disasters and emergencies, the maps help people understand the nature of these events.

Redhum:
http://www.redhum.org
OCHA administers this site, which provides easy, organized access to quality, up-to-date humanitarian information from Latin America.

PreventionWeb:
http://www.preventionweb.net/english
This site provides information on disaster reduction and humanitarian aid from the United Nations Inter-Agency Secretariat of the International Strategy for Disaster Reduction (ISDR).

Child Rights Information Network (CRIN):
http://www.crin.org/index.asp
The CRIN site provides information on children's rights by country and contains links to specific themes, such as armed conflict and the Convention on the Rights of the Child.

CRIN for Children:
http://www.crin.org/forchildren/index.asp

CRIN Resources:
http://www.crin.org/resources/treaties/index.asp
For searches of treaties and documentation relating to the rights of children, use the CRIN search function.

Save the Children
International Web site:
http://www.savethechildren.net

United Kingdom Web site:
http://www.savethechildren.org.uk/en/50_74.htm

Canadian Web site:
http://www.savethechildren.ca/index.html

U.S. Web site:
http://www.savethechildren.org

youthXchange:
http://www.youthxchange.net

Facts and Figures:
http://www.youthxchange.net/main/factsandfigures.asp
This youthXchange Web page provides information on the homeless and street kids.

World Values Survey:
http://www.worldvaluessurvey.org
This site provides information from many countries on the views held by the people there about the ideal number of children in their countries. (This data also appears at http://www.swivel.com/data_sets/columns/1016200.)

Youth Advocate Program (YAP) International:
http://www.yapi.org
The YAP International Web site contains information on ways to end child labor, children in armed conflict, exploitation of children and the imprisonment of children as adults.

Kid's Page: Opportunity to Learn:
http://www.yapi.org/kids/learn.htm

Right To Play International:
http://www.righttoplay.com
This site provides information about games around the world and Right To Play's efforts to help children worldwide develop skills, improve their health and resolve conflicts through sport and play.

The CIA World Factbook:
https://www.cia.gov/library/publications/the-world-factbook/index.html
Administered by the Central Intelligence Agency, this Web site provides information on every aspect of the world's countries and on other entities and dependencies.

Print Sources:
U.S. Central Intelligence Agency, *CIA World Factbook*, Skyhorse Publishing, New York, 2009 (and earlier editions published by Potomac Books, Dulles, VA).

The World Bank, *World Development Report*, Oxford University Press and The World Bank, Washington, DC, 2009 (and earlier editions).

The World Bank, *World Development Indicators*, World Bank Publications, Washington, DC, 2009 (and earlier editions).

United Nations Department of Economic and Social Affairs, *World Population Prospects*, United Nations, New York (various years 1998 – 2008).

World Health Organization, *World Health Report*, United Nations World Health Organization, New York, 1998 – 2008.

The Worldwatch Institute, *State of the World*, W.W. Norton, New York, 2009 (and earlier editions).